透明水彩で描く建築パース

鳥瞰図、外観図、インテリア

ハヤシスタヂオ 著

WATERCOLOR RENDERING

Exterior & Interior Perspectives, Bird'seye View

by HAYASHI STUDIO

透明水彩で描く建築パース

鳥瞰図、外観図、インテリア

Watercolor Rendering
—Exterior & Interior Perspectives, Bird's eye View—

Copyright by Hayashi Studio©
Published by Graphic-sha Publishing Co., Ltd.©
1-9-12 Kudan-kita Chiyoda-ku Tokyo 102 Japan
Phone: 3 3263 4318

ISBN4-7661-0643-1

English translation by James Fukuda
Printed in Japan by Kinmei Printing Co., Ltd.

First printing: August 1991

目 次

CONTENTS

本書のねらい

　昨今のはげしい技術革新のなかで，特にコンピューター技術の進歩には，めざましいものがあります。このためコンピューター・グラフィックによるパースの制作が年々盛んになる傾向にあります。

　しかし，また感性の時代と言われていて，その作品がアートの名に耐え得るようなパース技術もますます大切に思います。

　透明水彩で描く建築パースを紹介するために，表現技術の制作過程を，思いつくまま記述します。

　作品の打合せは，建築設計者及び各デザイナーなどの設計意図を的確に把握し，作品をどのように表現したいか検討します。アングルの決定は，頭の中で立体的に創作し，また同時にその場でイメージスケッチを描きながら話し合います。

　図面に基き正確な透視図をトレシングペーパーに描きます。透視図の中に，人間，樹木，車などを視点の高さに合わせて描き入れます。この状態で青図に何枚か撮って，各設計者側と打合せます。この時点で，全体の再チェックをしながら，材料や色を最終的に決定し，それに従い作品をつくります。

　インクは，カラーインク及び黒インクを使用します。素材の表現をリアルにするため，素材に合せた（大理石，タイル，木目，布地など）カラーインク作りが必要です。インキングが終った状態で，全体の40％の出来上がりを感じます。黒インクは，アウトラインに使います。

　透明水彩絵具は，非常にデリケートな絵具であり，その性質をよく知ることが必要です。絵具の性質は，植物性・鉱物性に分かれていますが，うまく組合せて混ぜることにより微妙な色彩が生まれます。茶系は鉱物性が多く，赤・青・緑系は植物性が主で，ウィンザーニュートン（イギリス製）のローズマダーなどは，花の香りがします。ウィンザーニュートンの水彩絵具は，発色と水彩紙へののりがよいです。

　それに透明水彩絵具の素晴らしさは，水加減で無限の色が出せることです。塗り込んでいくうちに，紙と絵具と筆加減で，非常にしっとりした仕上りになります。紙はアルシェ水彩紙（フランス製）が最高です。

　次に，素材に忠実な色づくりをし，素材に合わせて色見本をつくります。全体にそれぞれの色を塗り込み，より表現したい部分とおさえる部分を考えながら，色のコントラストを重要視して仕上げていきます。数多くのパースを制作する過程でテクニックの開発，発見などがあります。

　筆は，中から大は，ウィンザーニュートン（イギリス製），細筆は不朽堂の長穂白狸を使い，ロットリングは，0.1mm，0.2mm，0.3mmを使用します。

　プレゼンテーションが終った後は，その作品がアートとして残っていくことを念願し，そのためには，よい作品をつくるように心掛けております。私の今日までの作品の一部をご覧いただければ幸いです。

　作品には，建築物名称，設計者，制作年，鳥瞰，外観，内観の区別とサイズ(mm)を記してあります。

The Aims of "WATERCOLOR RENDERING"

In an age where technological innovations are being widely adopted, the progress being made in computer technology has been particutarly spectacular. It is no wonder that the use of computer graphics for creating perspective architectural designs is becoming more commonplace than ever.

However, we are also an age in which man's esthetic sense begs to be satisfied. Consequently, it is becoming increasingly important that perspective drawings be created so that they can also be called "works of art."

In these pages, I will describe the latest techniques and processes designers use and must go through when using transparent water colors to create perspective drawings.

Architectural designers and other designers must first decide on the image they wish to project and then determine how the perspective drawing will effectively convey that particular image. Designers conjure the three-dimensional angles in their minds and then produce image sketches to convey their ideas.

On tracing, paper, the designers then produce true-to-scale perspective designs according to plan. They draw human figures, trees, cars and other objects in scale to supplement the principal image. Consultations continue with each member of the design team armed with a copy of the blueprint. At this point, the team rechecks the overall plan and decides on the materials to be adopted and the principal color tone to apply. The final design is based on the decisions made at this stage.

For inking, black ink and colored inks are used. Ink colors are adjusted to give the materials (marble, tiles, wood, fabrics and others) used in the design a true-to-life look. When the respective colors have been inked in, about 40% of the perspective design work will have been completed. Black ink is used for drawing outlines.

A designer must understand the inherent features of transparent water colors since they are extremely "delicate" in nature. Although water colors are classified as either vegetable—or mineral—based, subtle, "delicate" color tones can be derived by applying them in coordinated combinations or in mixed form. A mineral-based color is suitable for brown tones. On the other hand, vegetable-based colors are best for red, blue and green tones. The aroma of flowers can be derived by using rose madder and other materials offered under the Winsor & Newton brand (made in Great Britain). Winsor & Newton water colors are excellent for color development and use with papers made for water coloring.

An outstanding feature of transparent watercolors is their capacity to produce unlimited color tones by increasing or reducing water admixture. As such, the designer can produce soft, refined finishes to the perceptive drawing by selecting the right paper and applying heavy or subdued brush strokes, as required, Arches brand water color papers (made in France) are excellent.

To reproduce the exact colors of the materials, the designer first makes different color samples. The designer then applies the colors to the materials, and finishes up the perspective design by creating the necessary color contrasts in the coloring process. In creating percetive designs, the designer discovers new ideas and learns to develop hands-on applications and techniques.

As for medium and large size brushes, those bearing the Winsor Newton brand are best; for small size brushes, the Nagaho Shirodanuki of Fukyudo (made in Japan) is ideal. Rotrings in 0.1mm, 0.2mm, and 0.3mm are used.

The designer must always aim to produce the best perspective drawing he can possibly create if wishes his work to be remembered as a work of art.

In these pages, I am showing some of the perspective designs I created over the years. I shall be very pleased if they will serve as a guideline to the readers of this book.

The name of the project, the designer, production date, bird's eye view, external plan, interior plan and the dimensions of the design are noted under each perspective design.

(仮称)西戸山高層住宅
Nishitoyama Koso Jutaku (temporary name)

設計：新宿西戸山開発株式会社

723×540

1986

鳥瞰図 Bird'seye view

Designer : Shinjuku Nishitoyama Development Co., Ltd.

Hayashi

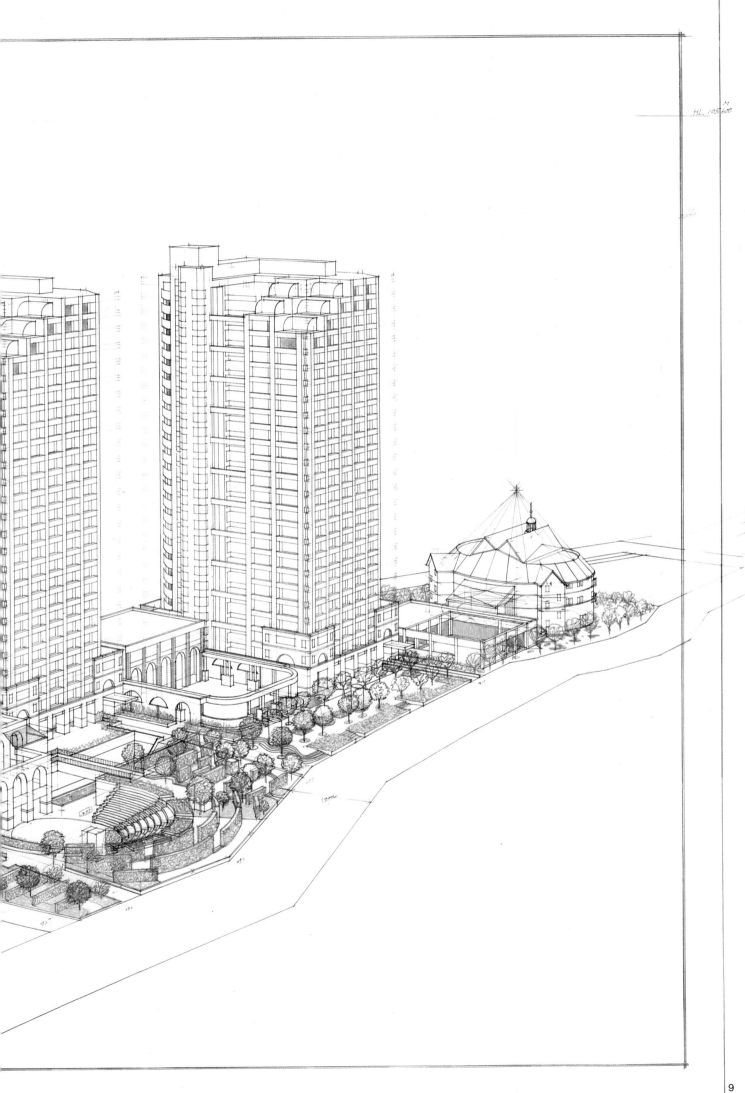

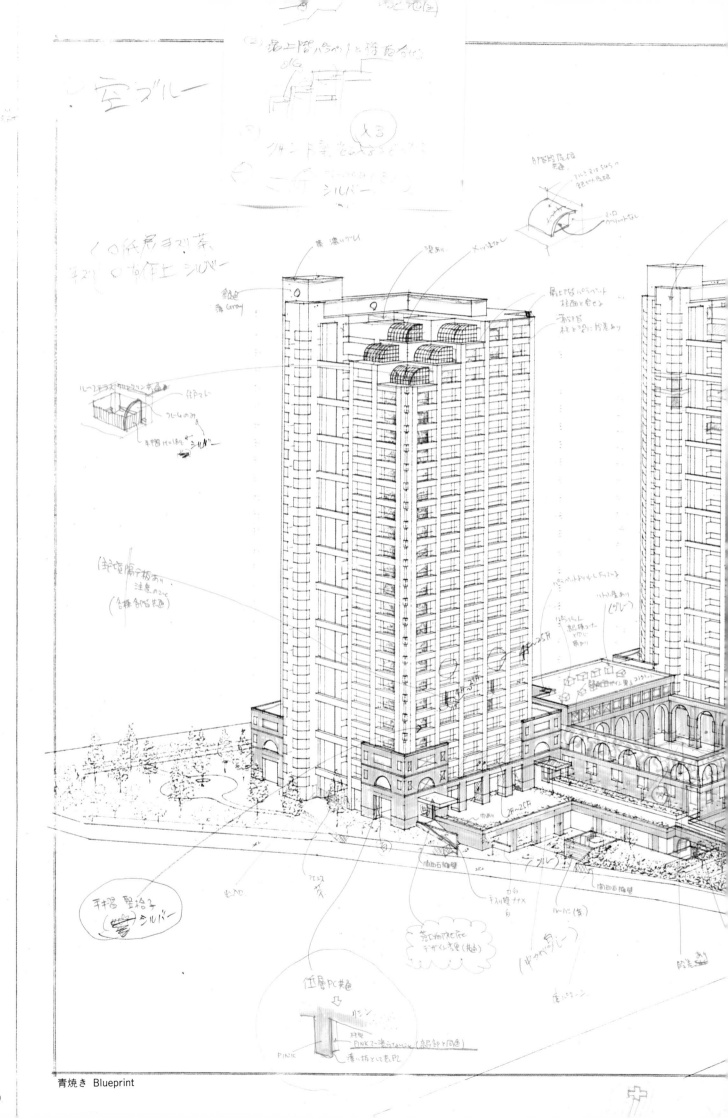

青焼き Blueprint

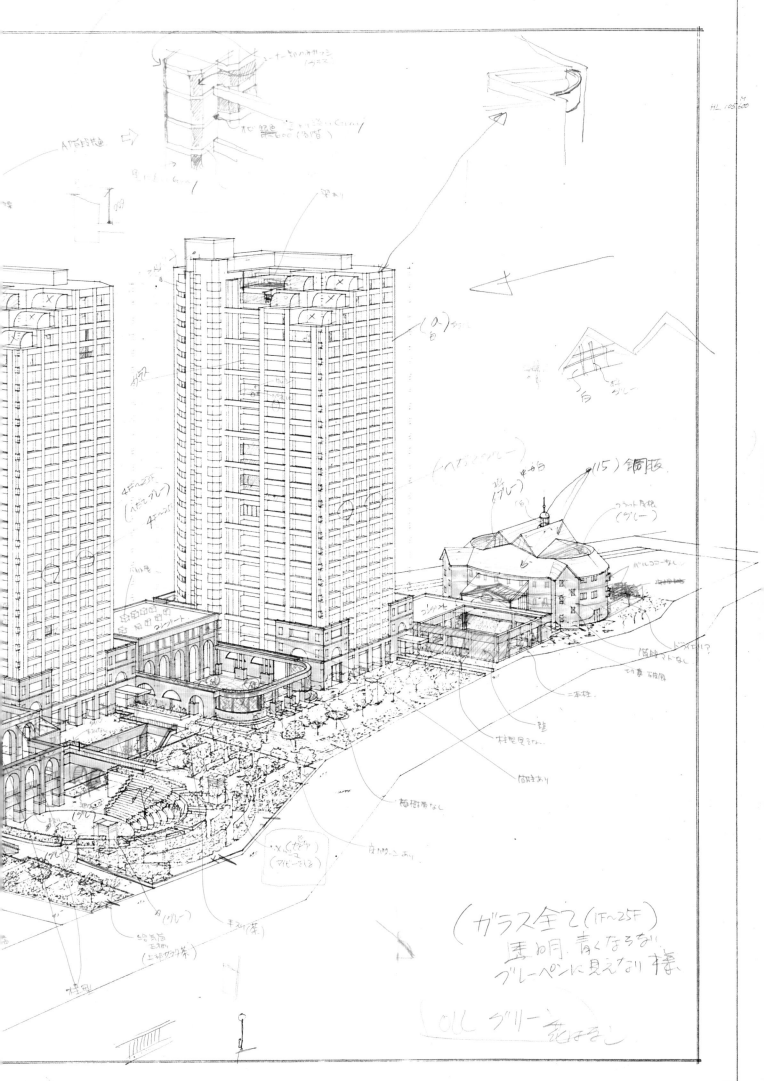

11

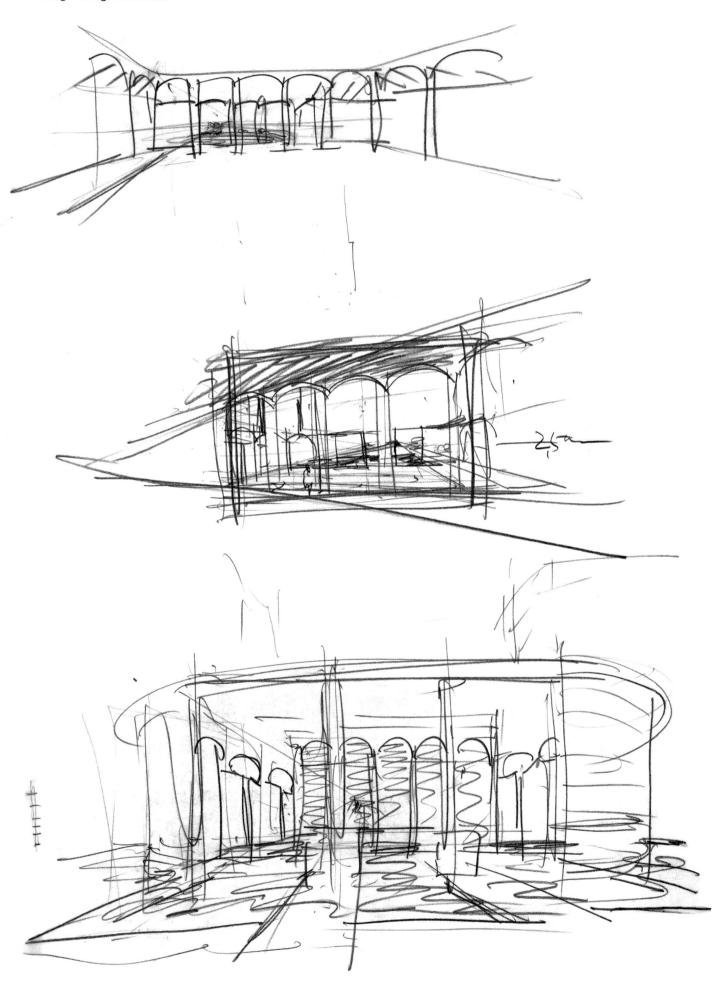

PLAZA-A ①

PLAZA-A ②

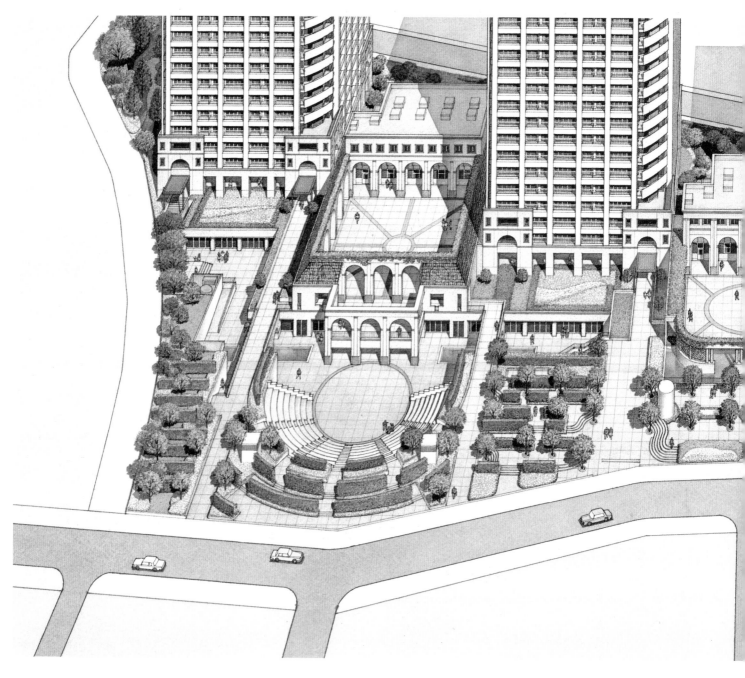

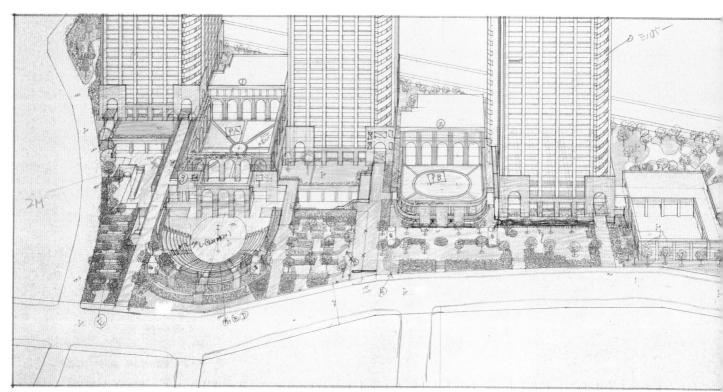

鳥瞰図 Bird'seye view 300×700

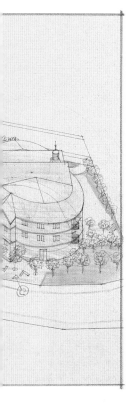

下図 Sketches

OUB CENTRE SINGAPORE

設計：丹下健三，都市・建築設計研究所
723×540
1982
外観図 Exterior plan

Designer : Kenzo Tange and
Urban Architects & Engineers

設計：三菱地所株式会社
1800×900
1968
外観図 Exterior plan

Designer : Mitsubishi Estate Co., Ltd.

世界一高層タワー計画案

Project plan of the world's highest tower.

イタリア　ペルージア市　都市計画国際コンペ「THE ASSEMBRI 71」
"THE ASSEMBRI 71," Town of Perugia (Italy) International Competition on Urban Planning

外観図 Exterior plan

ペルージア市の新市街地の再開発に関する都市計画国際コンペにおいて，１等入選作である。作品は，寸法が大きく建物が複雑なデザインであったために，３人で24時間続けて１ケ月もの時間がかった。さらに現地の雰囲気を出すために，添景にも時間を要した。

This design work captured top honors in an international competition on the redevelopment of an urban area of Perugia Town. Because of the design's large dimensions and complicated building forms, the three designers practically worked around the clock throughout a one month period. They also expended a great deal of time in order to successfully portray the town's local color into the design.

設計：早大「THE ASSEMBRI MOTTO W 4338」チーム名
池原義郎氏，木村傳氏，森義純氏ほか各氏
1800×850
1971

Designer : Waseda University "THE ASSEMBRI 71 MOTTO W 4338" Team (Yoshiro Ikehara, Tsutou Kimura, Yoshiizumi Mori and others)

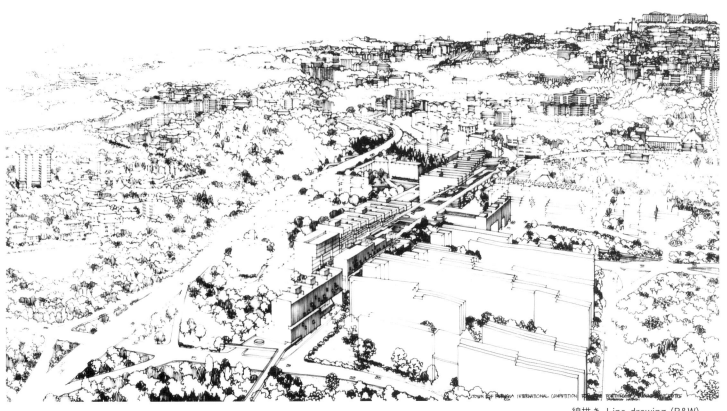

線描き Line drawing (B&W)

逆版（白黒反転）Reverse (white & black) exposures

本書の表紙は，この作品の線描きをもとにしたものである。
(0.5mm のフェルトペンを使用)

The cover of this book adopts the lines of this design work
(drawn with a 0.5mm felt pen) .

関西国際空港
Kansai International Airport

設計：長島建築研究所
723×540
1978

Designer :
NAGASHIMA ARCHITECTS

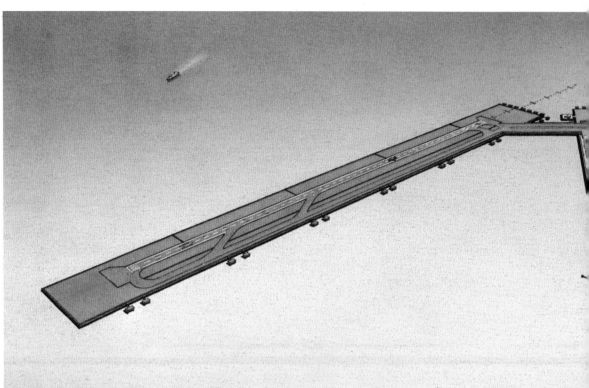

浮体工法による関西国際空港 B-2 案（新交通システム）（下層型待合室）
Floating Kansai International Airport, Plan "B-2" (new transportation system)
(underground waiting room) ▼

浮体工法による関西国際空港 Floating Kansai International Airport

浮体工法による関西国際空港 A 案（昇降式トランスポーター）
Floating Kansai International Airport, Plan "A" (escalator transporters)
723×540

GATE 27-32

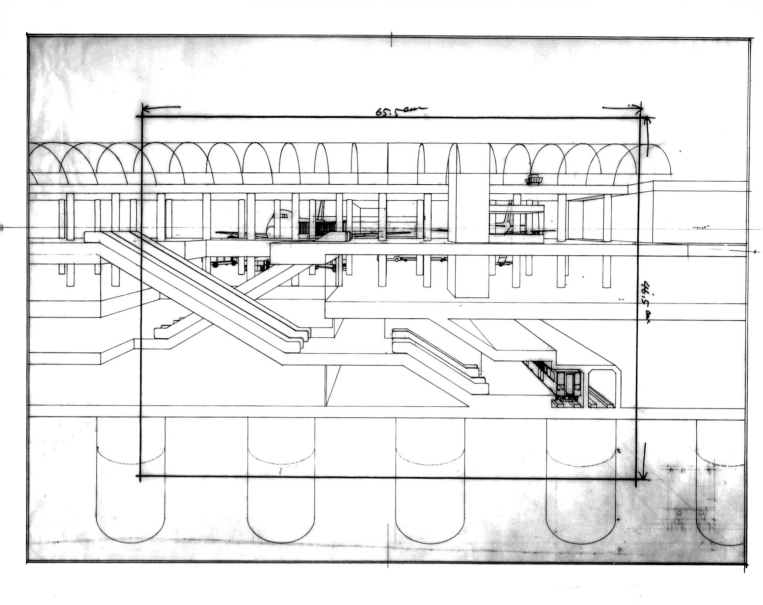

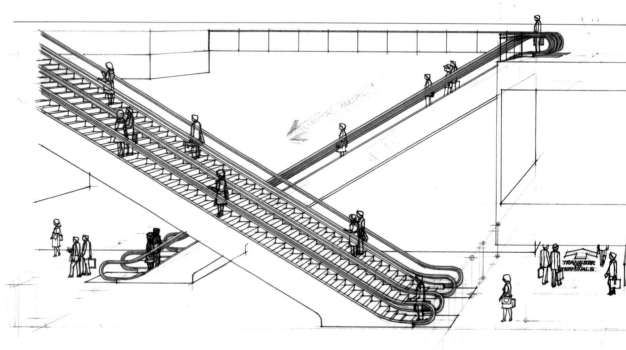

浮体工法による関西国際空港 B-I 案(新交通システム)(地上型待合室) 723×540
Floating Kansai International Airport, Plan "B-I" (new traffic system) (above-ground waiting room)

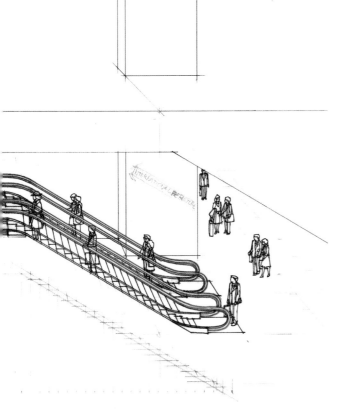

下図 Sketch

バグダッド国際空港計画案
Bagdhad International Airport Project Plan

設計：長島建築研究所
1977

Designer : NAGASHIMA ARCHITECTS
内観図 Interior plan (B&W) 841×594

内観図 Interior plan (B&W) 841×594

外観図 Exterior plan 723×540

内観図 Interior plan 723×540

28

内観図 Interior plan　723×540

(仮称)池袋計画案
Ikebukuro Project Plan (temporary name)

設計：三菱地所株式会社
723×540
1971

Designer : Mitsubishi Estate Co., Ltd.

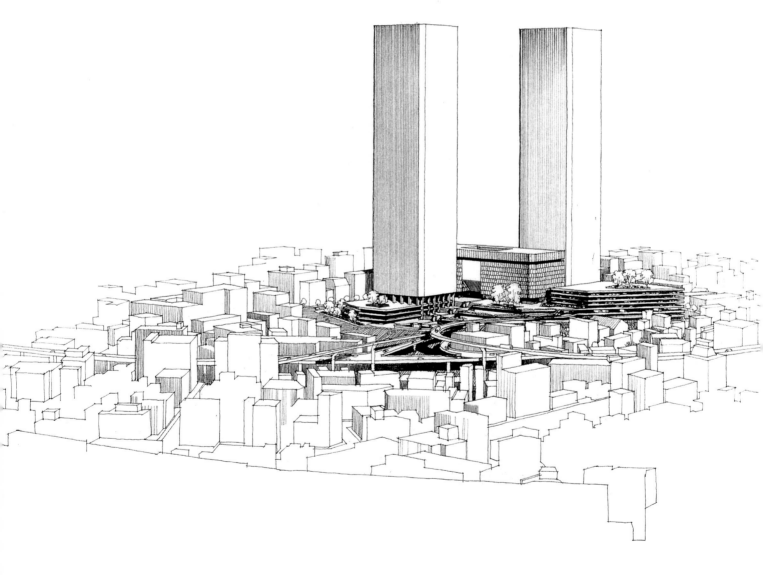

鉛筆（2 B）描きのアングルイメージ　723×540

Angle images drawn with 2B pencil.

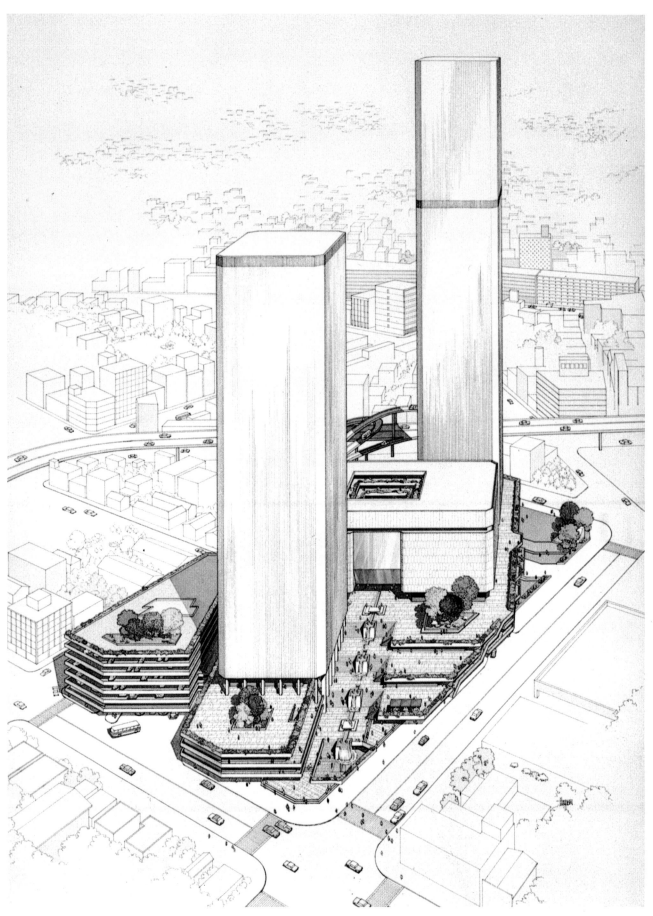

モノトーン Monotone 723×540

(仮称)JTC イン芦ノ湖
JTC Inn Ashinoko (temporary name)

鳥瞰図 Bird'seye view 723×540

エントランスアプローチ外観図 Entrance＋Approach/Exterior plan 545×425

断面図 Cross section 545×425

日本観光サービス（株）
設計：アトリエ RIX
1978

Japan Sightseeing Services Co., Ltd.
Designer : Arelier RIX

中庭ファサード外観図 Courtyard & Facade/Exterior plan 545×425

内観図 Interior plan 545×425

下図 Sketch

設計：森 義純＋(株)CORE 建築設計事務所

545×425

1980

外観図 Exterior plan

Designer：Y.MORI＋CORE Architects & Associates

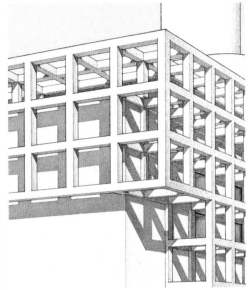

正確に立体感を表現するためには，影のつけ方は非常に重要である。光の角度や位置を想定し，正確に影のアウトラインを描くことによって，建物の構造のリアルさを出すことが出来る。さらに材質感を出すには，1～2度の塗りではなかなか出ないので，より効果を出すために，水彩絵具を重ね塗りすることによって，しっとりとした仕上がりになる。

The technique of drawing shadows is an important element in giving the design an accurate three-dimensional look. The structure of the buildings becomes true-to-life when the position of the sun is set and the outlines of the shadows are drawn in line with the angle of light. The quality of construction materials cannot be shown with just one or two coats of paint. In this case, the design's eye-catching, lucid finish was derived with many layers of watercolor coatings.

sumitomo U. HD-HC proj.

住友高層住宅計画案
Sumitomo U. HD-HQ
Project Plan

設計：
（株）木村傳建築設計事務所
1053×900
1969
鳥瞰図 Bird'seye view

Designer : Tsutou Kimura
Architects

大泉学園コミュニティセンター計画案
Oizumi Gakuen Community Center Project Plan

設計：（株）坂倉建築研究所
723×540
1979
鳥瞰図 Bird'seye view

Designer : SAKAKURA ASSOCIATES architects and engineers

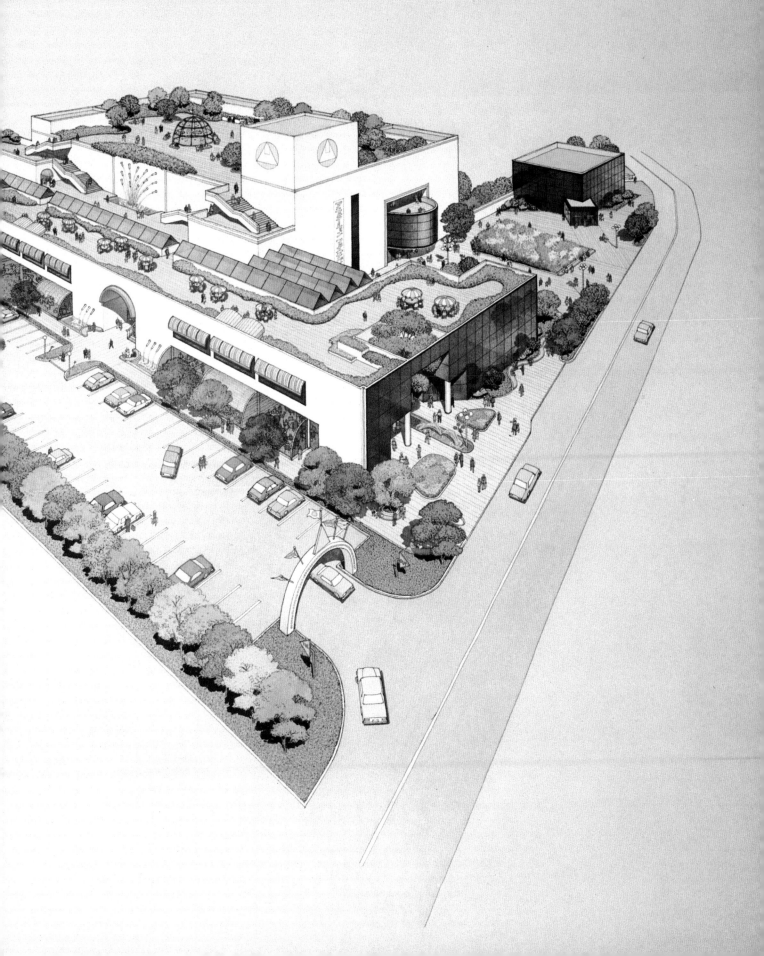

鳥瞰図 Bird'seye view 860×610

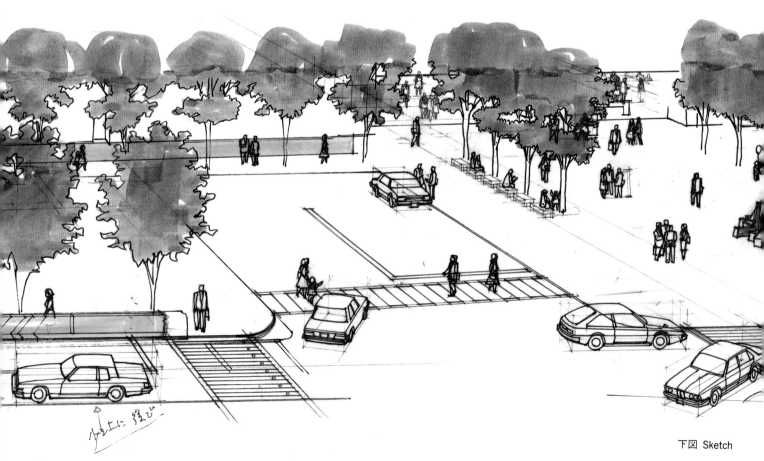

下図 Sketch

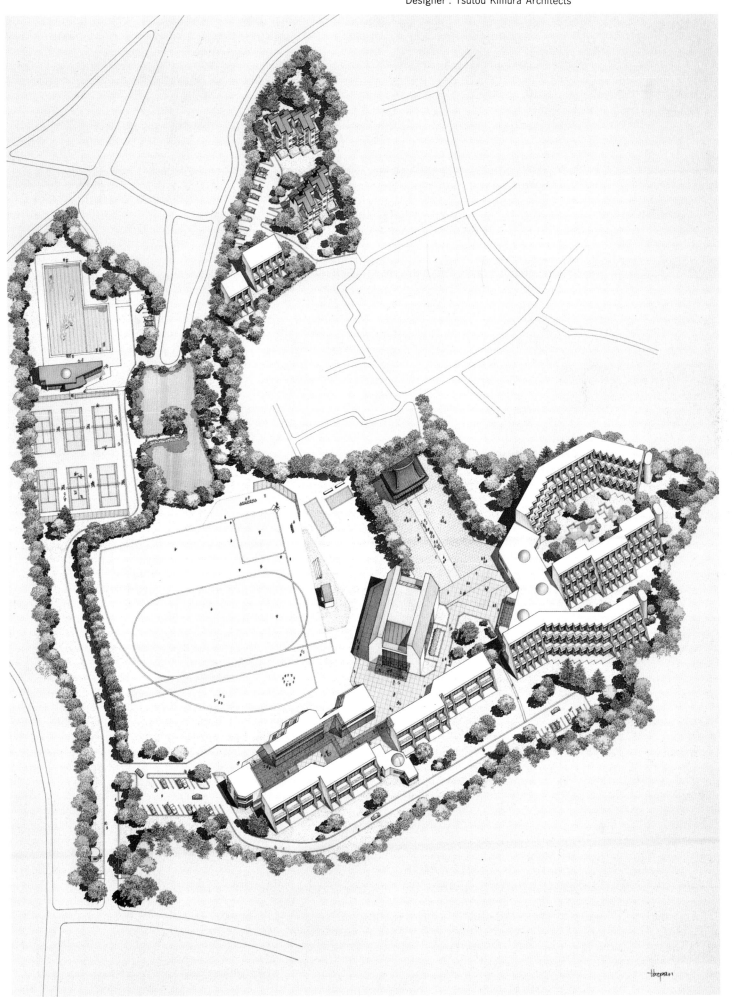

鳥瞰図　Bird'seye view　723×540

福岡市庁舎計画案
Fukuoka City Administration Building Project Plan

設計：(株)坂倉建築研究所

Designer : SAKAKURA ASSOCIATES architects and engineers
1979

外観図 Exterior plan 723×540

会議室 Conference room 545×425

中庭 Courtyard 545×425

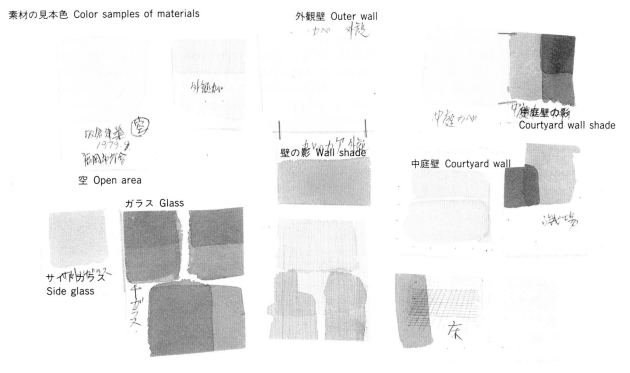

素材の見本色 Color samples of materials

外観壁 Outer wall

中庭壁の影
Courtyard wall shade

空 Open area

壁の影 Wall shade

中庭壁 Courtyard wall

ガラス Glass

サイドガラス
Side glass

床 Floor

川久保ビル
Kawakubo Building

設計：森 義純＋（株）CORE 建築設計事務所
545×425
1977

Designer：Y.MORI＋CORE Architect & Associates

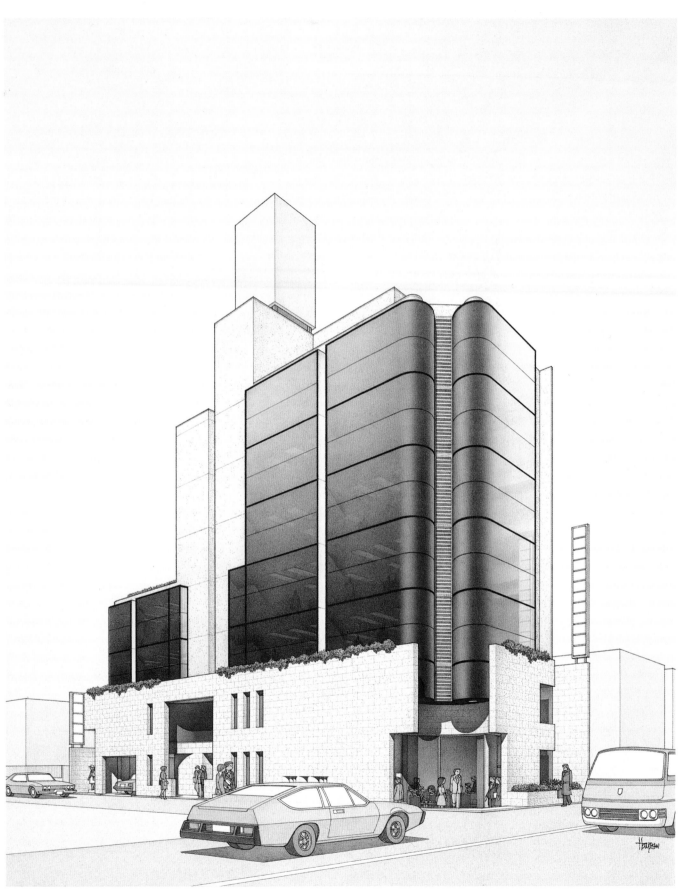

外観図 Exterior plan

設計：森 義純＋(株)CORE 建築設計事務所
545×425
1976

Designer：Y. MORI ＋ CORE Architect & Associates

建物のデザインをどう活かすか，ガラスのカーブを描くなどのテクニックに時間を要した。

外観図 Exterior plan

Design work entailed much time and technical effort in conveying the image of
the curved lines of the glass walls and windows to enliven the building's overall
design.

計画案外観図 Exterior plan

幕張海浜公園日本庭園茶室
Japanese Teahouse, Makuhari Seashore Park

設計：中畑建築設計事務所
723×540
1988

Designer: Nakahata Architects and Engineers

日本人でありながら，日本様式の建物を描く難しさを思い知った作品である。
それは，日本庭園であるとか，茶室の感じなど日頃ふれることが少ないため，
専門書で資料を集める。
瓦，柱，たたみ，木目などは，それぞれをよりリアルに表現することである。

This work shows the difficulty even a Japanese designer faces in
designing a traditional Japanese style building.
The designer usually relies on materials from books and other literature on Japanese architecture and design since Japanese parks and
rooms for traditional tea ceremonies are not part of his daily routine.
Roof tiles, wooden posts, wood grain, straw mats and other materials
must be conveyed in real-to-life appearance.

広間 Main hall　545×425

茶室　425×350
Tea ceremony room

レリアン・レナウンホームズ広尾マンション
Lillian Renown Homes Hiroo Mansion

設計：（株）日建設計
723×540
1982

Designer: Nikken Sekkei

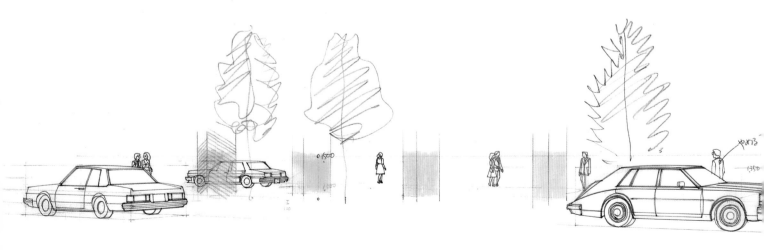

エントランスホール　Entrance hall　723×540

外観図　Exterior plan

エントランスホールより外を見る
Looking out from the entrance hall.

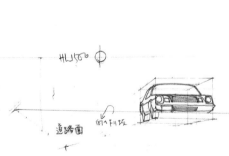

素材の見本色　Sample colors of materials

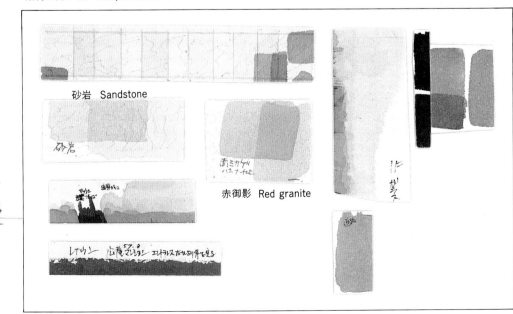

砂岩　Sandstone

赤御影　Red granite

富山県リハビリテーション専門病院基本計画案
Preliminary Basic Plan of the Toyama Prefecture Rehabilitation Hospital

設計：（株）共同建築設計事務所　1981
Designer: Kyodo Architects and Engineers

鳥瞰図　Bird's eye view　723×540

外来待合室　Outpatient waiting room 545×425

運動療法室　Rehabilitation exercise room 545×425

リハビリテーションの動きなどは，明るく表現する。病院関係の書物で，人物描写を間違うことのないよう注意した。

Patient rehabilitation work is expressed in a bright, cheerful manner. The designer was particularly careful to portray human forms accurately by referring to technical medical books and literature.

外観図 Exterior plan　723×540

計画案外観図　Preliminary exterior plan　723×540

第一勧業銀行
The Dai-Ichi Kangyo Bank, Ltd.

設計：芦原建築設計研究所
Designer: Ashihara Architects and Engineers
1976

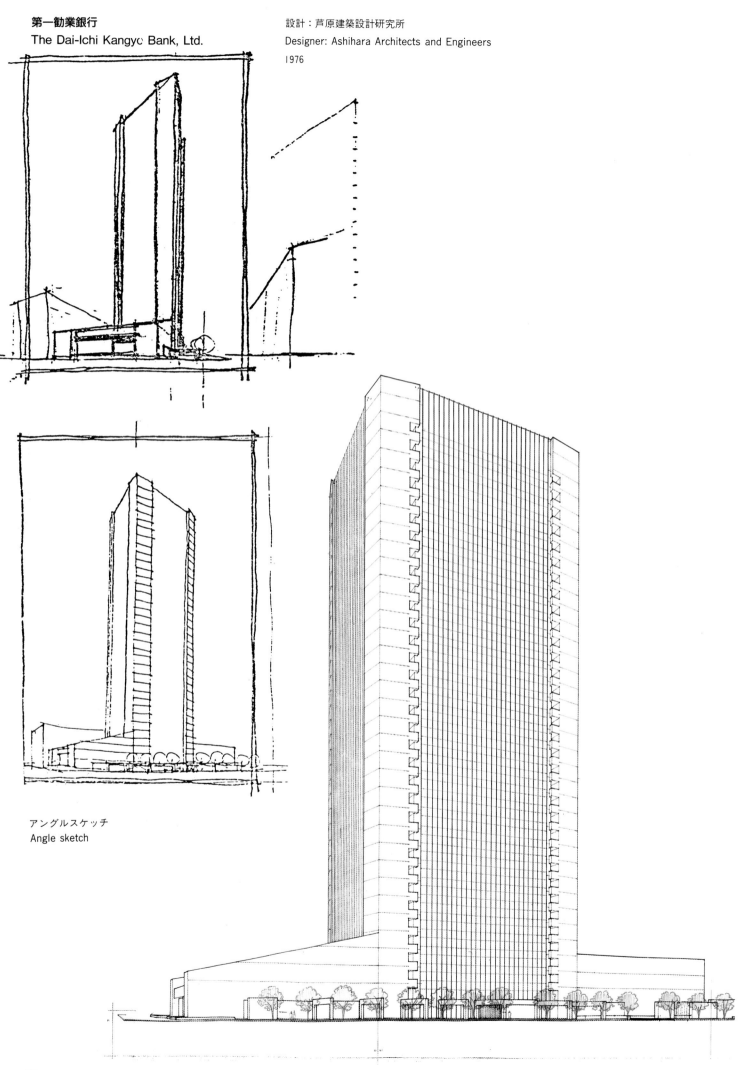

アングルスケッチ
Angle sketch

外観図 Exterior Plan 723×540

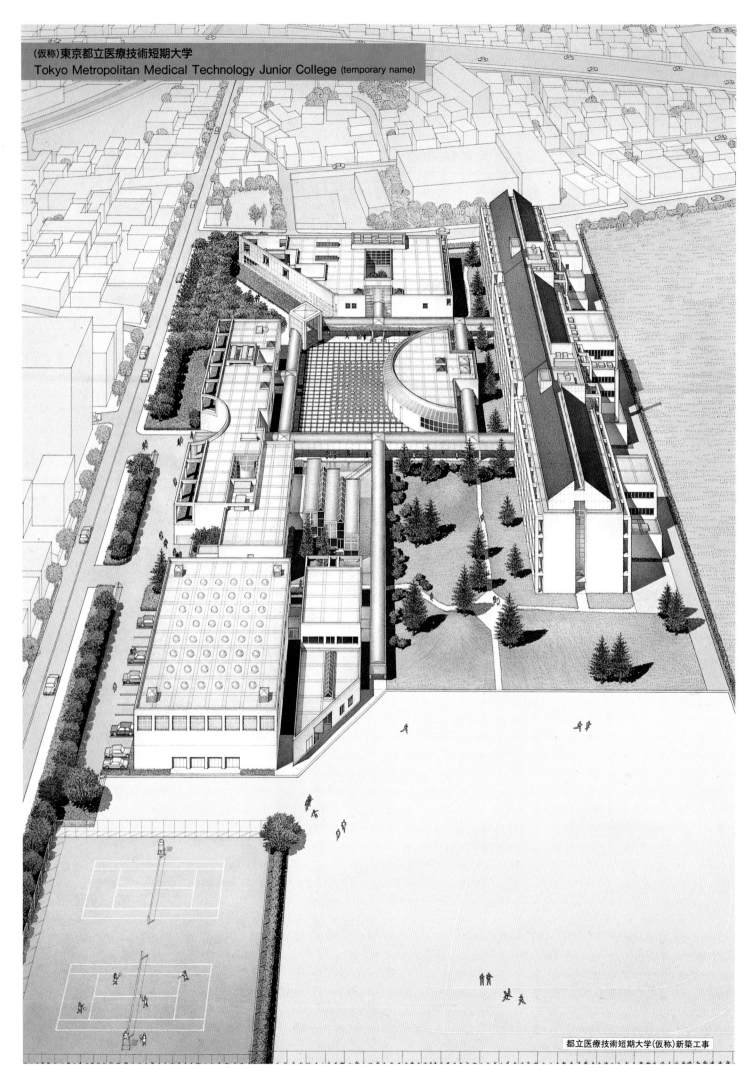

(仮称)東京都立医療技術短期大学
Tokyo Metropolitan Medical Technology Junior College (temporary name)

都立医療技術短期大学(仮称)新築工事

58

講堂 594×420
Auditorium

設計：（株）坂倉建築研究所
Designer: SAKAKURA ASSOCIATES architects and engineers
1984

鳥瞰図
Bird'seye view
594×420

(仮称)芳樹館

Hojukan (temporary name)

設計：森 義純＋(株)CORE 建築設計事務所
Designer：Y. MORI ＋ CORE Architect & Associates
1989

鳥瞰図　Bird'seye view　723×540

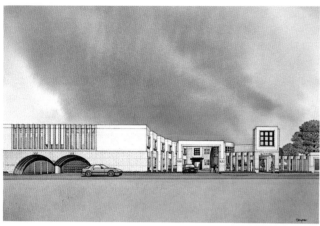

外観図　723×540
Exterior plan

建物のデザインが微妙にカーブしているので，透視図の
作画に時間を要した作品。

In this case, the designer had a difficult time in
producing the cut-away view because of the
building's delicate curves.

前橋市庁舎
Maebashi City Administration Building

設計：（株）坂倉建築研究所
Designer: SAKAKURA ASSOCIATES architects and engineers
1977

外観図 Exterior plan 723×540

(仮称)千葉県東総文化会館
Chiba Prefecture East Culture Center (temporary name)

設計：（株）前川建築設計事務所
Designer: Maekawa Architects and Engineers
1988

鳥瞰図 Bird'seye view 723×540

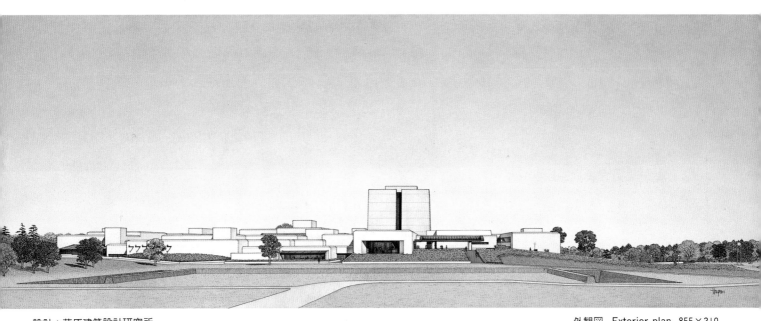

設計：芦原建築設計研究所
Designer: Ashihara Architects and Engineers
1977

外観図　Exterior plan　855×310

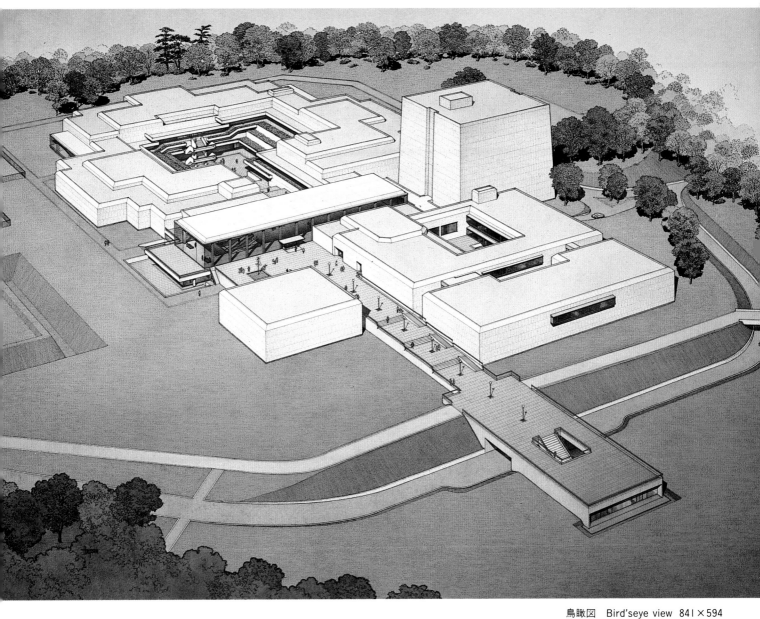

鳥瞰図　Bird'seye view　841×594

大洋漁業
Taiyo Fishery Co., Ltd.

外観図（B） Exterior plan(B) 723×540

設計：(株)松田 平田 坂本設計事務所
Designer: MATSUDA HIRATA SAKAMOTO ARCHITECTS/
　　　　　　PLANNERS/ENGINEERS
1975

第1案では，設計通りの材質感を出して仕上げた(A)。第2案は，皇居に鶴が舞いおりたイメージを表現する事を要望された為に，白く清楚な作品となる(B)。

テクニックとして，ブラックインク30%グレーにして建物を描いた。

Plan #1 (A) was finished with a hue, according to the original design, to depict the quality of wood. Plan #2(B) was transformed into a clean white design from a request to convey the image of storks swimming in the Imperial moat, in the building's foreground.

The technique involved was to finish the building with a gray hue (containing 30% black ink).

外観図(A) Exterior plan (A) 723×540

直井ガーデンビル
Naoi Garden Building

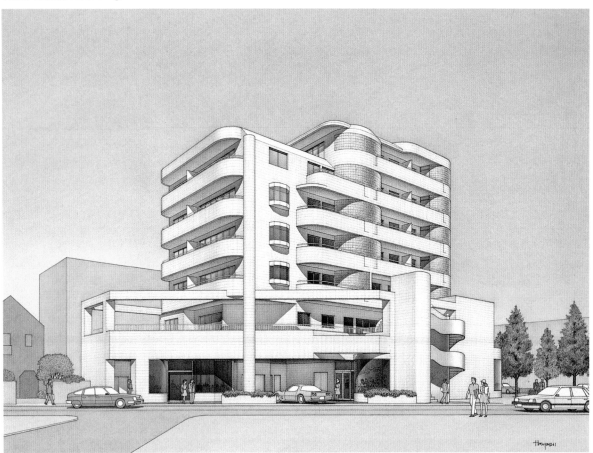

設計：(株)KIA 都市，
　　　建築研究所
545×425
1986
外観図 Exterior plan

Designer : KIA Urban
Architects

株式会社兼アーバン虎の門ビル
Ken Urban Toranomon Building

設計：(株)堀江，阿部
　　　総合計画事務所
723×540
1985
外観図 Exterior plan

Designer : Horie and Abe
General Planners

設計：(株)アートボックス▶
　　　建築設計工務
723×540
1985
外観図 Exterior plan

Designer : Art Box Architects
and Engineers

京橋トキワビルⅡ
KYOBASHI TOKIWA BLDG2

設計：(株)KT 建築研究所　1986

Designer : KT ARCHITECTS & ASSOCIATES

外観図　Exterior plan　545×425

設計：(株)KT 建築研究所　1987
Designer : KT ARCHITECTS & ASSOCIATES

外観図 Exterior plan 545×425

覚張ビルディング
GAKUHARI BUILDING

横浜人形の家
Yokohama Doll Museum

設計：(株)坂倉建築研究所　1984

Designer : SAKAKURA ASSOCIATES architects and engineers

外観図 Exterior plan 545×425

素材の見本色 Color samples of materials

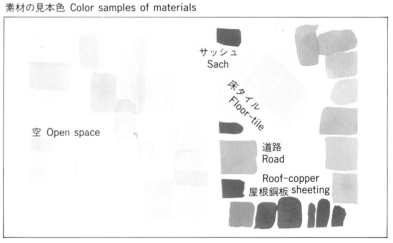

空 Open space

サッシュ
Sach

床タイル
Floor-tile

道路
Road

Roof-copper
屋根銅板 sheeting

実景
Actual view

鳥瞰図 Bird'seye view 723×540

設計：マスタアズ建築企画
1982

Designer : Masters Architect and Planning

設計：森 義純＋（株）CORE 建築設計事務所
545×425
1987
正面外観図 Exterior plan, front view

Designer：Y.MORI＋CORE Architect & Associates

左：地域センター
右：オフィスへの入り口
Left: Community center
Right: Office complex entrance

外観図 Exterior plan 545×425

断面図 Cross section 545×425

ヤマギワ　ストリートマップ
Yamagiwa Street Map

鳥瞰図　Bird'seye view 950×740
1984

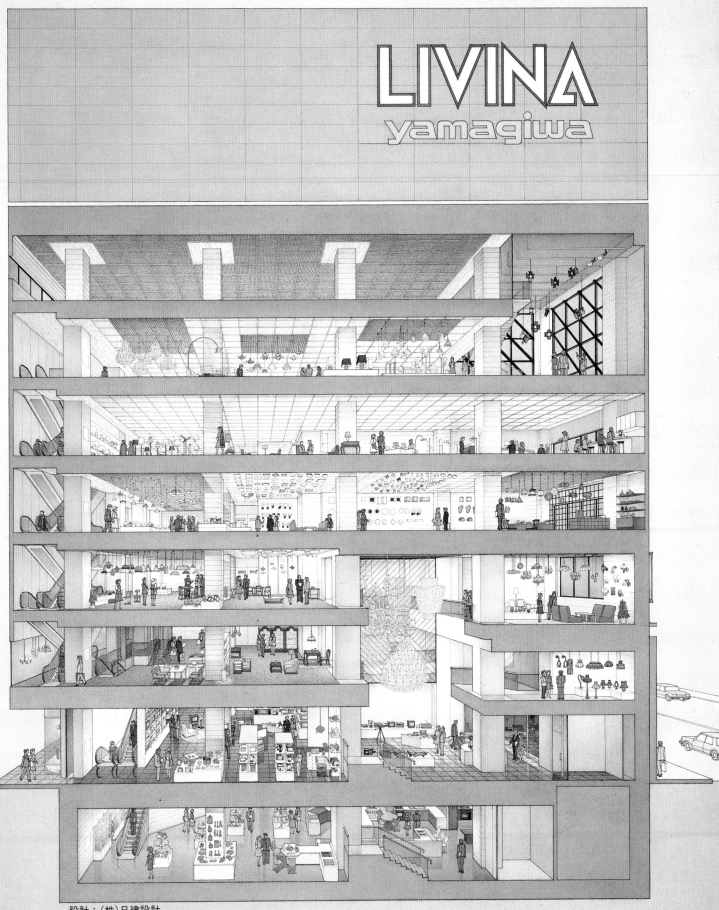

LIVINA
yamagiwa

設計：（株）日建設計

Designer : Nikken Sekkei Ltd.

1983

断面図　Cross section　723×540

このバスは隣との関係とのバランス？

アクセントカラー？

女子学生会館スペランザ　クニタチ
Speranza Kunitachi College Woman's Hall

基本計画：日本食品株式会社

意匠：ハヤシスタヂオ

Basic planning : Nihon Shokuhin Co., Ltd.

Design : Hayashi Studio

1986

外観図 Exterior plan 723×540

実景　Actual view

エントランス Entrance 545×425

実景 Actual view

スピーレンⅡ
Spielen Ⅱ

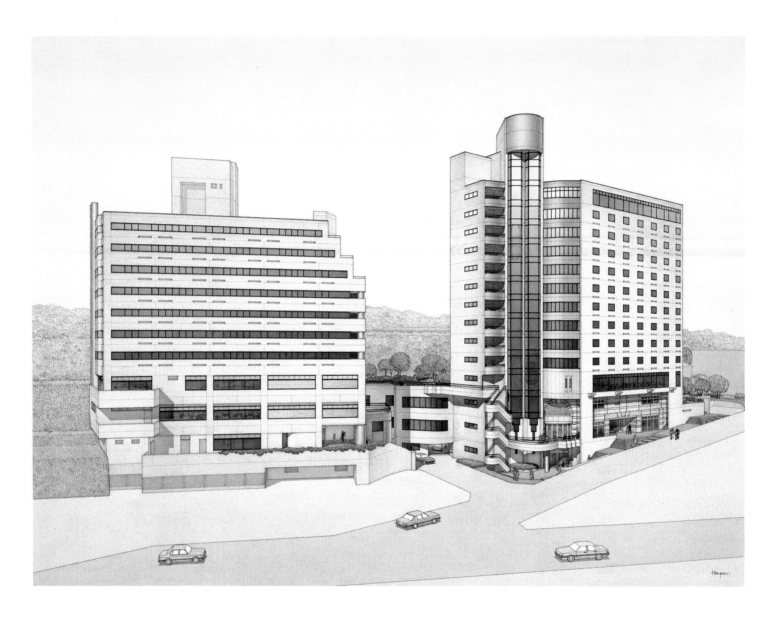

設計：(株)木村傳建築設計事務所

723×540

1987

外観図 Exterior plan

Designer : Tsutou Kimura Architects

設計：（株）木村傳建築設計事務所
545×425
1984
鳥瞰図（B＆W）Bird'seye view (B&W)

Designer : Tsutou Kimura Architects

代官山パークサイドビレッジ
Daikanyama Parkside Village

設計：㈱KT 建築研究所

Designer：KT ARCHITECTS & ASSOCIATES
1981

外観図 Exterior plan 700×300

ファサード
Facade
545×350

コーヒーショップ Coffee shop 425×350

リビング Living room 425×350

オフィス Office 425×350

パールツリー新町
Pearl Tree Shinmachi

設計：森 義純＋（株）CORE 建築設計事務所

Designer：Y.MORI＋CORE Architect & Associates
1986

設計：森 義純＋（株）CORE 建築設計事務所

外観図 Exterior plan 545×425

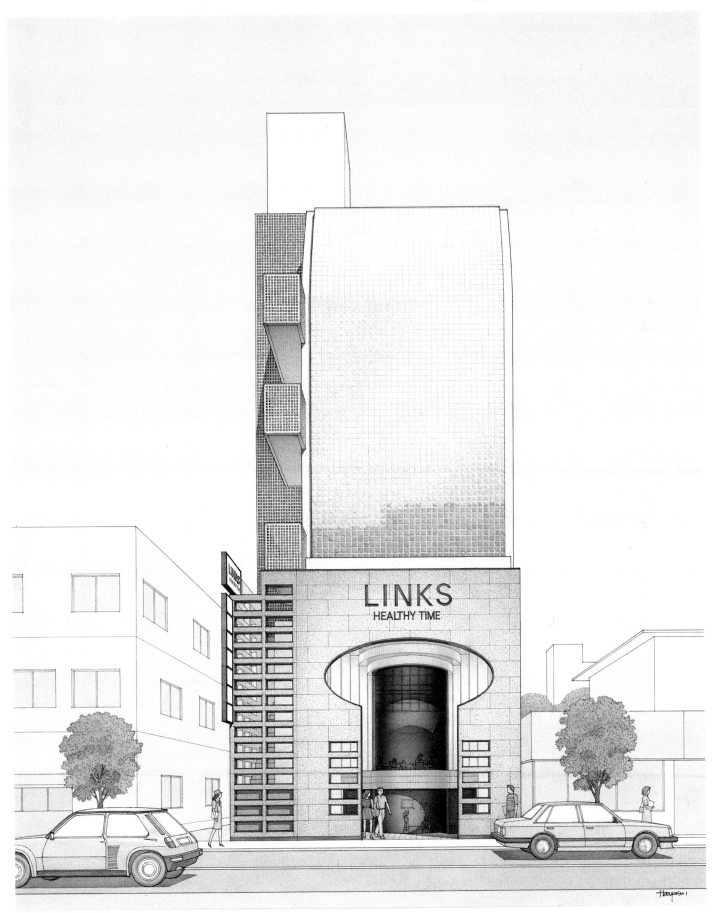

外観図 Exterior plan 545×425

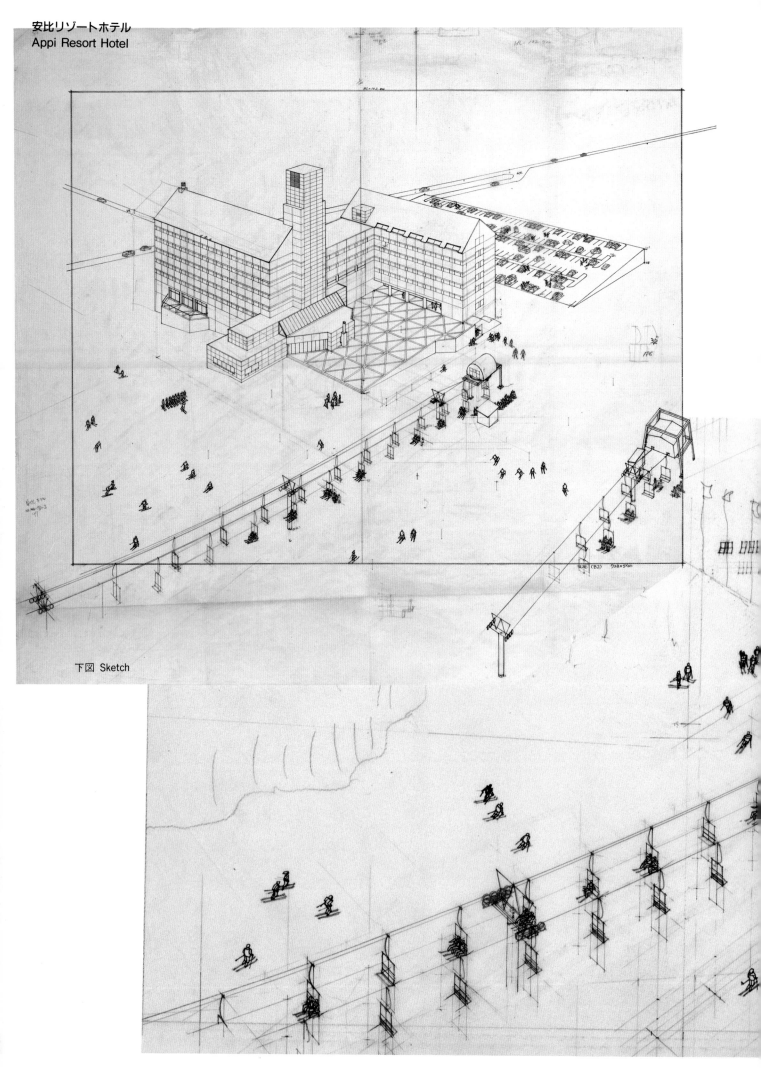

下図 Sketch

設計：谷口建築設計研究所

Designer : Taniguchi Architects and
    Engineers

1984

鳥瞰図 Bird'seye view 723×540

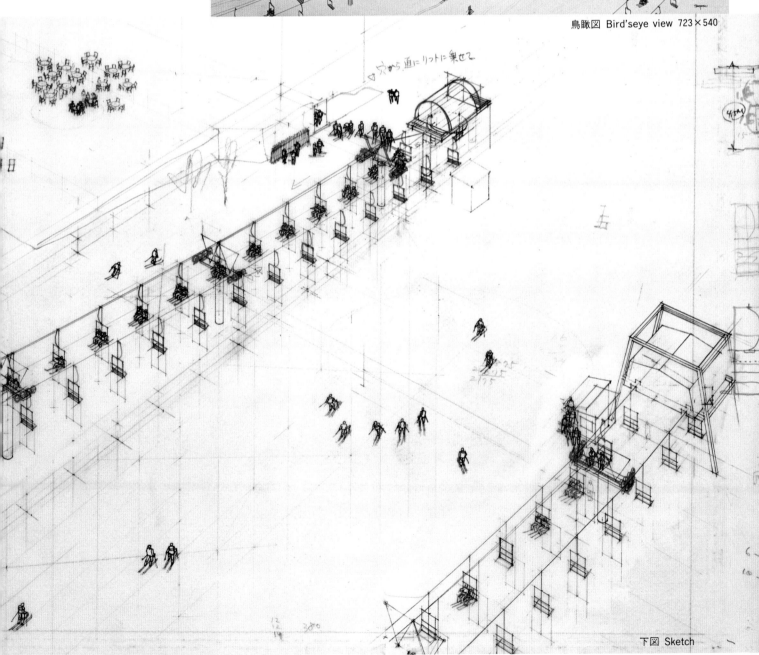

下図 Sketch

レストラン Restaurant 425×350

ティーラウンジ Tea lounge 425×350

ロビー Lobby 425×350

新宿ワシントンホテルアネックス
Shinjuku Washington Hotel Annex

設計：(株)坂倉建築研究所

Designer : SAKAKURA ASSOCIATES
architects and engineers
1985

外観図 Exterior plan
723×540

会議室 Meeting room 425×350

パーティルーム Party room 425×350

ロビー Lobby 425×350

新宿ワシントンホテル新館
Shinjuku Washington Hotel Shinkan

設計：(株)坂倉建築研究所

Designer：SAKAKURA ASSOCIATES architects and engineers
1985

ステーキレストラン Steak restaurant 425×350

スイートルーム Suite room 425×350

ティーラウンジ Tea lounge 425×350

インテリアの表現は，デザインされた空間をいかに描くか重要である。そのためには，床，壁，天井それぞれの面はもとより，ファニチャー，人物，小物類などの寸法は正確でなくてはならない。

それは，色，型，パターン，素材(木目，敷物，布地など)，質感，着彩のコントラストにより，高さ，広がり，奥行きなどデザインされた空間を一目瞭然に見せることが出来る。

How one fills the open space of a design is an important factor in providing a vivid look to the interior design. The appearance and dimensions of the floor, wall, ceiling, as with furniture, people and objects, should be drawn as true-to-life as possible for effect.

The height, width and depth of design of open space can be immediately projected by using distinctive color, shapes and patterns and by providing a sense of contrast to the quality and appearance of the materials (wood, carpets, cloths) used.

新宿ワシントンホテル
Shinjuku Washington Hotel

ティーラウンジ Tea lounge　425×350

設計：（株）坂倉建築研究所

Designer : SAKAKURA ASSOCIATES
architects and engineers
1983

ロビー Lobby　425×350

藤の椅子を表現するには，寸法，型，色，こ
れら全てを忠実に描き，透して見える向側の
デザインを正確に描くことにより，リアルさ
を増すことになる。

The atmosphere of rattan chairs is
heightened if they appear true to size,
shape and color and the design in the
background is shown accurately
through the rattan's wall of transpar-
ency.

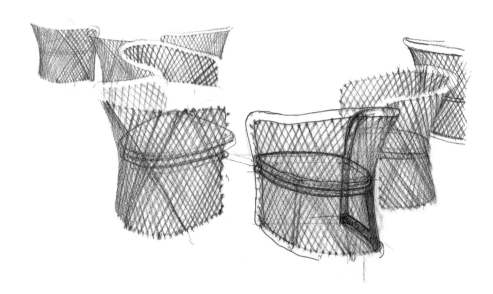

和風レストラン Japanese restaurant 425×350

バー Bar 425×350

パブレストラン Pub restaurant 425×350

かごしま林田ホテル
Kagoshima Hayashida Hotel

ガーデンテラス Garden terrace 545×425

パーティルーム Party room 700×300

メインロビー Main lobby 700×300

カクテルバー Cocktail bar 700×300

設計：前原誠デザイン室

Designer：Makoto Maehara Design Office
1974

コーヒーショップ Coffee shop 700×300

日本料理店 Japanese restaurant 700×300

前ページのガーデンテラスは，4面がハーフミラーで設計されている
ため，天井のトラスなど，見えるものすべてが無限に映る。したが
って制作に4週間ぐらい時間を要した。

The design shown on the foregoing page adopts half
mirrors on all four sides to create a sence of unlimited
space in the garden terrace ceiling trusses as well. A period
of roughly four weeks was required to create such an effect
in the design.

中華料理店 Chinese restaurant 545×425

フランスレストラン French restaurant 545×425

会議室 Meeting room 545×425

結婚式場 Wedding hall 545×425

ビアレストラン
Beer hall and restaurant

デザイン：ハヤシスタヂオ

Designer : Hayashi Studio
1976

内観図 Interior plan 700×300

BEER RESTAURANT DESIGN : Papsh

伊東泉郷プラザホテル （株）いずみごう
Ito Izumigo Plaza Hotel

設計：（株）レーモンド設計事務所

Designer : Raymond Architectural Design Office, Inc.
1985

鳥瞰図 Bird'seye view 723×540

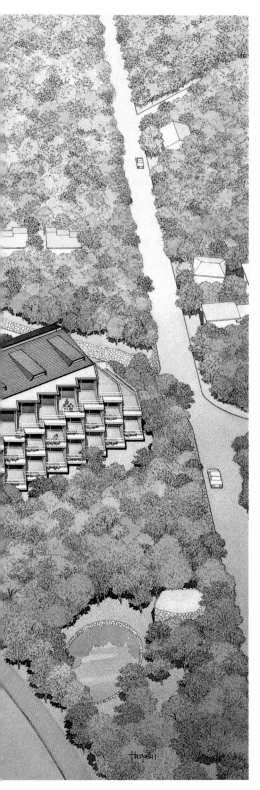

ロビー Lobby 545×425

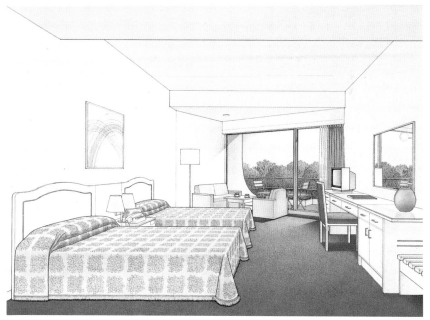

客室 Hotel room 425×350

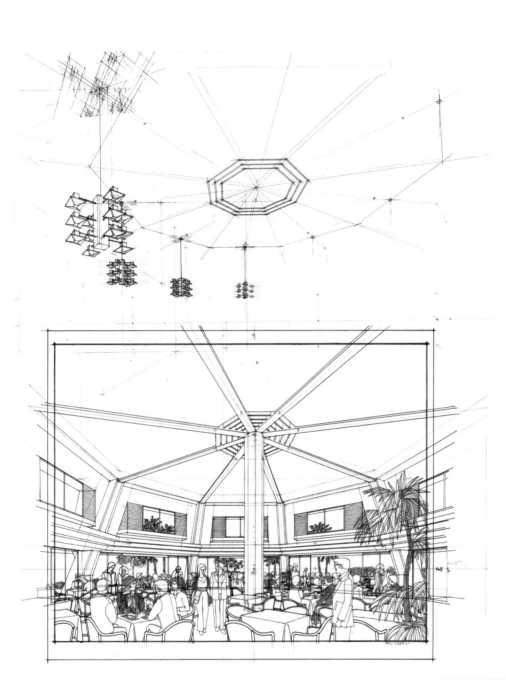

レストラン Restaurant 545×425

下図 Sketch

青焼き Blueprint

積水ハウス株式会社　都市開発事業部
設計：エストエンジニアリング（株）

Sekisui House Ltd.
Designer : EST Engineering Co., Ltd.
1990

鳥瞰図 Bird'seye view 723×540

下図 Sketch

外観図 Exterior plan 545×425

オークタウン船橋
Oak Town Funabashi

設計：(株)大蔵屋

Designer : Okuraya
1981

鳥瞰図 Bird'seye view 920×680

住宅外観 Exterior plan of single unit 545×425

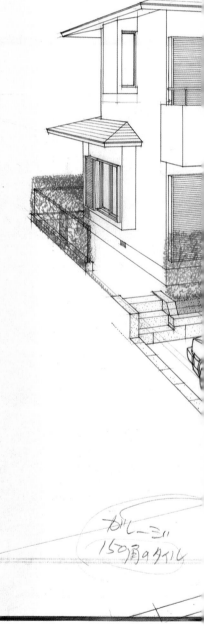

がレージ
150角のタイル

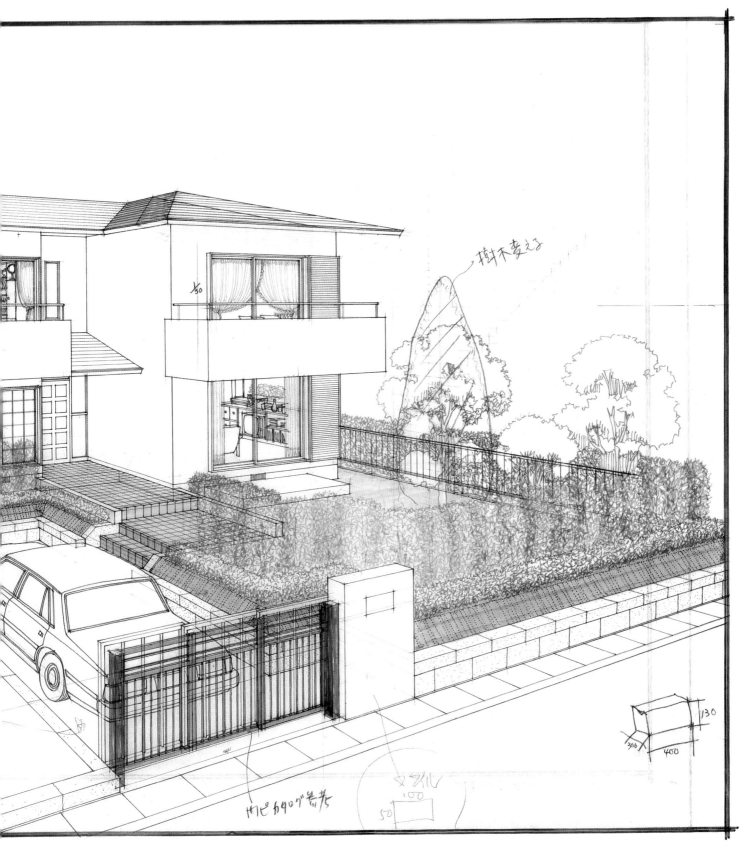

樹木変える

130
300 400

タイル
100
50

サピ カタログ参照

リビング Living room 545×425

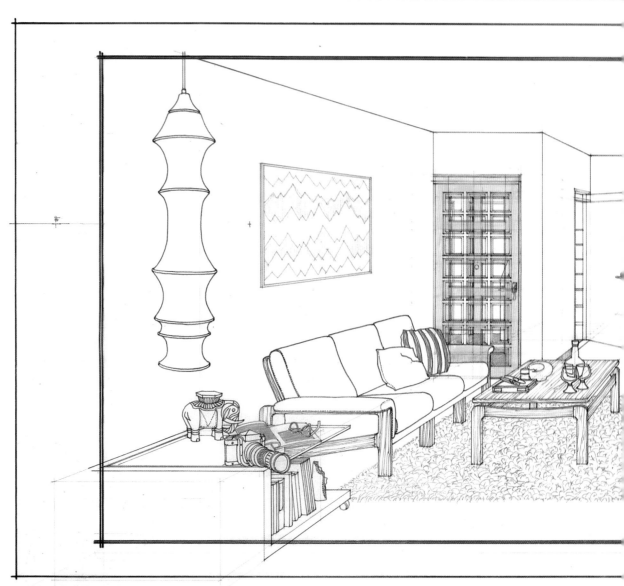

H.h 1.5h

カットライン

フレームライン

TYPE B-10 700×300 Hayashi Studio

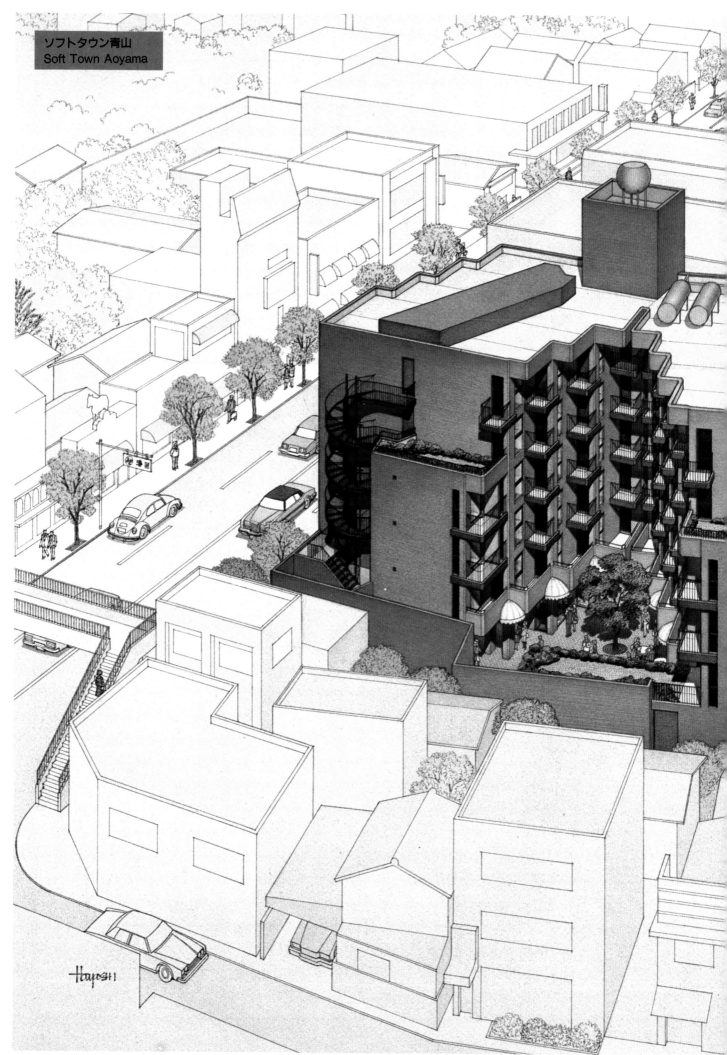

ソフトタウン青山
Soft Town Aoyama

鳥瞰図 Bird'seye view 723×540

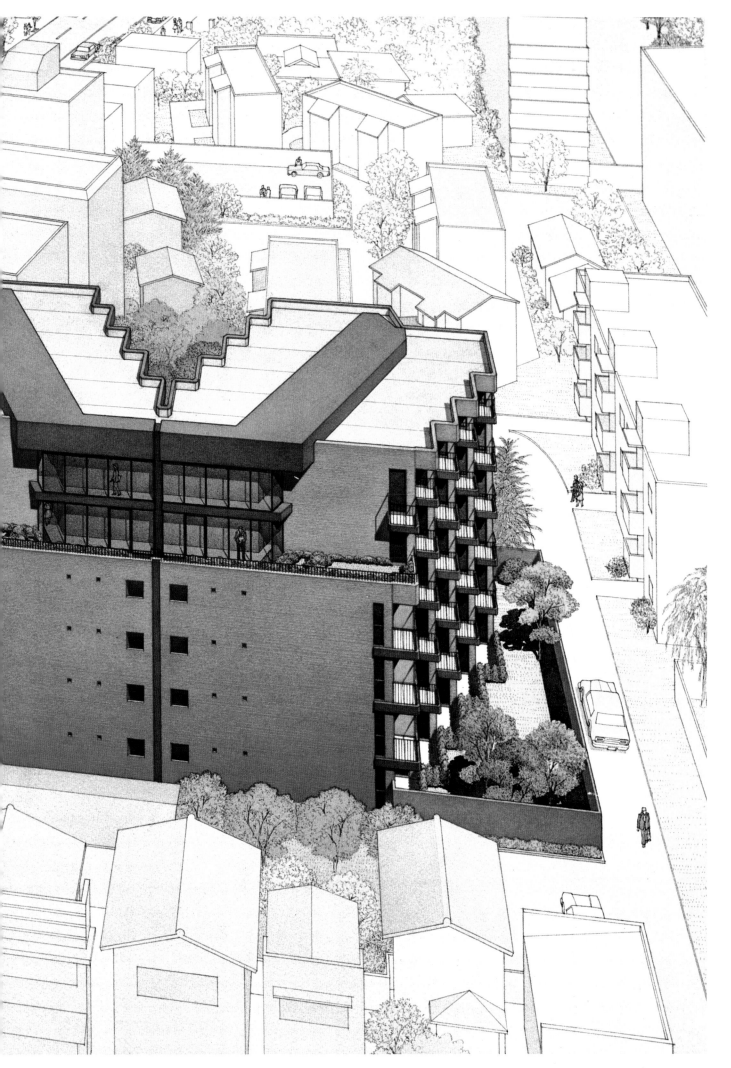

設計：建築総合計画研究所

Designer : KENCHIKU SOGO KEIKAKU KENKYUJO
1978

外観図 Exterior plan 545×425

素材の見本色　Color sample of materials

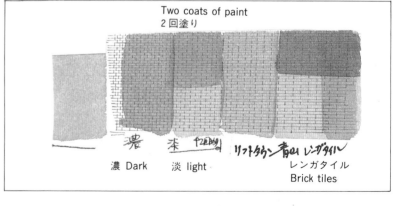

Two coats of paint
2回塗り

濃 Dark　　淡 light

リフトタウン青山 レンガタイル
レンガタイル
Brick tiles

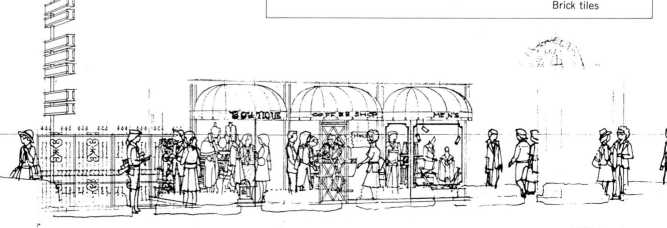

下図 Sketch

ショッピングプラザ Shopping plaza 545×425

グリーンプラザ
Green plaza

545×425

リゾートハウス集合住宅
Resort House Shugo Residence

（株）アサヒプランニングアート

Asahi Planning Art
1973

鳥瞰図 Bird'seye view 1000×700

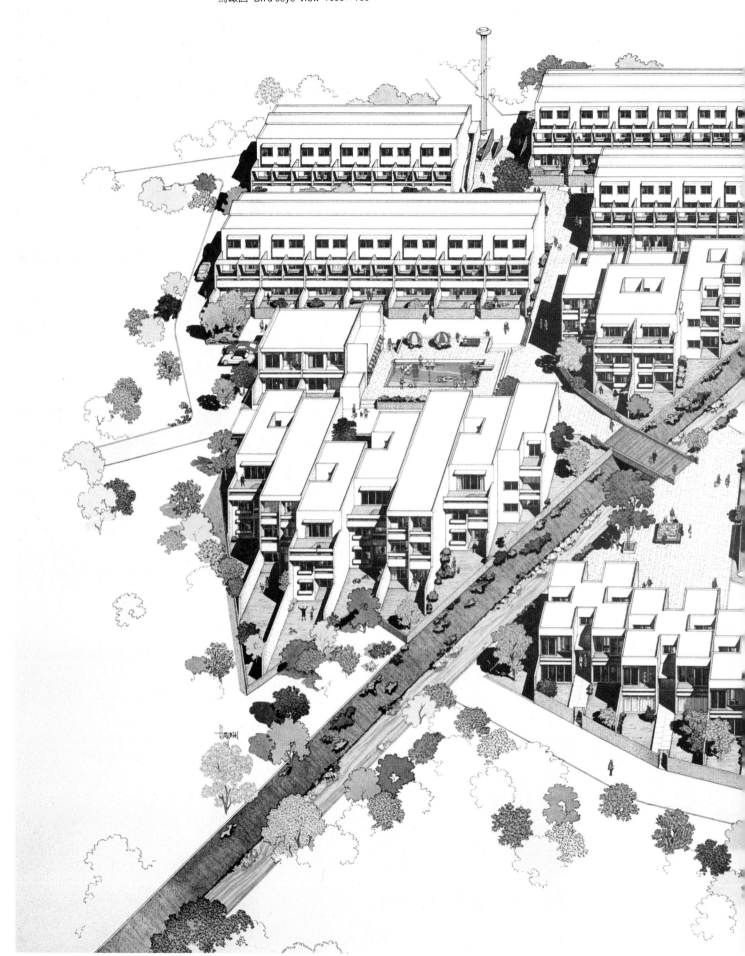

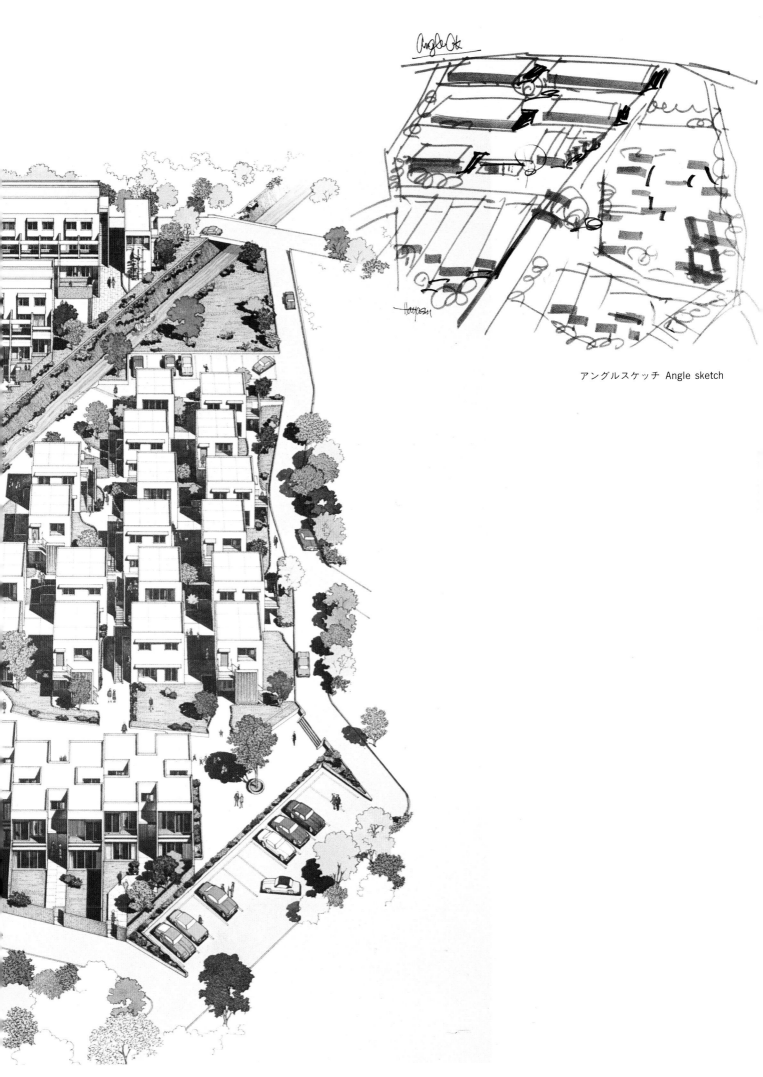

アングルスケッチ Angle sketch

133

グランドメゾン津田沼
Grand Maison Tsudanuma

積水ハウス株式会社

Sekisui House Ltd.

1986

鳥瞰図 Bird'seye view 723×540

積水ハウス株式会社

Sekisui House Ltd.
1982

外観図 Exterior plan 723×540

臼杵市 開発ニュータウン
Usuki City New Town

設計：森 義純＋（株）CORE 建築設計事務所　1974
Designer：Y.MORI＋CORE Architect & Associates

ハイツ成城
Heights Seijo

積水ハウス株式会社
723×540
1985
鳥瞰図 Bird'seye view

Sekisui House Ltd.

設計：保坂陽一郎建築研究所
545×425
1986
鳥瞰図　Bird'seye view

Designer : YOICHIRO HOSAKA ARCHITECT & ASSOCIATES

塚本ビル
Tsukamoto Building

設計：三菱地所株式会社

Designer : Mitsubishi Estate Co., Ltd.

1971

外観図
昼景
723×540

Exterior plan,
daytime

外観図
夜景
723×540

Exterior plan,
nighttime

設計：保坂陽一郎建築研究所
545×425
1986
外観図 Exterior plan

Designer : YOICHIRO HOSAKA ARCHITECT & ASSOCIATES

実景 Actual view

石原裕次郎邸
Residence of Yujiro Ishihara

設計：(株)松田 平田 坂本設計事務所
545×425
1980
外観図 Exterior plan

Designer : MATSUDA HIRATA SAKAMOTO ARCHITECTS/
PLANNERS/ENGINEERS

設計：(株)池原義郎・建築設計事務所
723×540
1989
外観図 Exterior plan

Designer : Yoshiro Ikehara Architect & Planning

著者紹介

株式会社 ハヤシスタヂオ
〒186 東京都国立市西2丁目8番地の11
電話(0425)72-7784

林 陸紀
1941：神戸出身

Profile

Hayashi Studio

2-8-11, Nishi, Kunitachi-shi, Tokyo 186 Japan
Phone: (0425) 72-7784

Mutsunori Hayashi
Born in 1941, Kobe-city.

翻訳：ジェイムス福田
Translation by James Fukuda

透明水彩で描く建築パース
Watercolor Rendering
—Exterior & Interior Perspectives, Bird's eye View—

1991年8月25日　初版第1刷発行

著　者　ハヤシスタヂオ©
発行者　久世利郎
印刷所　錦明印刷株式会社
製本所　大口製本株式会社
写　植　三和写真工芸株式会社
発行所　株式会社グラフィック社
　　　　〒102 東京都千代田区九段北1-9-12
　　　　電話 03-3263-4318　振替 東京3-114345
落丁・乱丁はお取替え致します。

ISBN4-7661-0643-1 C3052